aleš mustar

c(o)urt in

Frankfurters, frankfurters, frankfurters.

Frankfurters all the time.
Burnt for breakfast,
smoked for lunch,
grilled for dinner.

Frankfurters, frankfurters, frankfurters.

As I close my eyes
and fall into sweet sleep, frankfurters crawl into my dreams.

Frankfurters, frankfurters, frankfurters.

Žiga Mohorič, 3rd grade pupil, Idrija Primary School, Slovenia

BLATT BOOKS

ISBN 1-59971-339-X

Book & cover design by Mario Dzurila (studio@blatt.cz)

Some of these translations originally appeared in the following print and electronic publications, occasionally in a different form: *BLATT*, *Blesok*, *3am Magazine*, *Absinthe*, *Gloom Cupboard*, and *Sawbuck*.
Thanks to all those editors.

www.blatt.cz

BLATT BOOKS are distributed by Small Press Distribution:
www.spdbooks.org.

aleš mustar

c(o)urt interpretations

translated from the slovenian by manja maksimovič

The first collection of poems by Aleš Mustar, who previously published his work in several Slovene and international magazines, opens up a number of issues related to poetry's so-called engagement as well as the poet's dethronement from the laws of aesthetics. As a court interpreter, Mustar is able to perceive the present and the laws of the capitalistic world more thoroughly; as a translator, he grasps both the internal and external parts of language; and as a poet, he attempts to capture fundamental existential experience on paper. The line from the poem "Go West" – "Real-life stories" – says it best. It can be interpreted as the author's principal credo: he writes down stories as they happen in real life. Indeed, the material for his poetry is life itself, yet it is often lifted from the ground by the poetic process and set adrift to imaginary landscapes like a balloon on a string. In this respect, Mustar's emergence in the Slovene literary milieu is a breath of fresh air. Above all, it is a multilayered starting-point that accounts for his ethical-moral-legal standing, which is in part reflected in this collection. However, to expect Mustar's collection to be a simple legal code containing articles and paragraphs, prohibitions and commands for the poets and the nation, would be in vain. Even sparser in Mustar's poetry are traces of self-pity or an emphasis on tragic human existence. This is due to the poet's wide angle, which encompasses all levels of human existence. Deep inside, in spite of his broad experience and maturity, the poet still clings to the asides of an outcast who is the only one capable of recognizing the face of truth in the muffled game of cultural patterns and habits.

robert simonišek
aleš mustar's poetry of revolt

Mustar's poetic subject, the poet himself, faces everyday problems with bravery and energy. In his poetry, Mustar does nothing to conceal his errors of judgment and would not be caught idealizing anything without a cogent reason. As a writer, he is situated in the capital of Slovenia, which provides an external frame for most of his poems. The actuality in which Mustar depicts fragments of his life fades away when faced with the supreme issues of successfully saving the world (in the introductory poem "Depression": "Should I turn into Super, Action or Spiderman, / are you willing to become my Xena / so that together we can save the world?") and of responsibility towards reality and other people. Mustar thus simultaneously banters and criticizes his own life, and even more so the surrounding Slovene society, its rules, laws of communication and its essence. Contrary to many Slovene poets, Mustar does not build his poems on the aesthetics of the language, lyricism or pathos, nor does he glorify his role as a messenger or place the poet in the role of a shaman. In Mustar's view, the poet's position is not a superior one, that of "a godsend to the earth"; rather, he faces the destinies of time with his ordinary bloodshed eyes of a mortal. With considerable vehemence, Mustar takes the opposite approach, which surpasses the message of a provocation, seemingly invariable in form. In his poems, the poet is thus more often a dehumanized than a glorified figure (as in the poem "At the Red Snake": "There are no manners at the Red Snake, you can eat with your fingers. / The poet sentenced to silence is brought innards.") Since in the modern world of Mustar's poetry, hope and trust in distinguished and eminent values are undermined, the poetic language adequately turns rustic, while the contents acquire a consumerist nature. Yet once Mustar denounces "the poetic ego" in a flourish, he is bound to bring it back in a different, more "revolutionary" manner (in "Crime and Punishment," for instance, the poet calls on imaginary protagonists of Dostoevsky's novel to join him for a glass of vodka). On occasion, Mustar gives the impression that an ironic smirk is one of the best means in a struggle against the indecent and sometimes even senseless world which moves away from the subject with a megalomaniac speed, instills in him the sense of emptiness, and encourages a "Don Quixotic state of mind," woven through and through with the skepticism of a modern intellectual.

Speaking of form, the poet approaches prose poetry, using a language similar to that used in street conversation. As to the contents, the schism between the poet, his role in the society, and reality is strongly evident in Mustar's poetry, while the author's internal, psychological struggle, indicated by the descriptions of his physical and psychological condition, is set to become its permanent subject matter. In the poem "Diagnosis," the poet introduces us to his physical condition and health. Similarly, the theme of the poem "Airborne" is the poet's body, examined by a physician. This poem may be a paradigmatic example of the (infinite) extent to which Mustar would go to intensify an event from his real life. On the other hand, the psychological struggle brings forth schizophrenic ideas with no solid foundations that the author fully acknowledges and uses as a filter (from the poem "Literary Nocturne": "Drink up the Biokill and kill the night moths, / give me a knife so I can rip up my belly / and twist Jonah's neck.") The author sets himself the task to realize and "heal" his own faults through poetry. In some poems, "the Sartresque crushing atmosphere of anxiety" ends with a romantic cliché exclamation ("Environmental Poem.") In "Nostalgia," the poet, after initial observation, gets lost in the images of protagonists and poets from different periods in world literature, which is another open display of his sympathy for literature. The author is fully aware of literary legacy, which can have a positive effect or can be merely a troublesome nuisance (as in the poem "Legacy.") Mustar rarely succumbs to mysterious erotic outbursts in his poems; on the contrary, he portrays this emotion with the existential sensitivity of a man trying to approach a woman, more often than not with a heavy dose of cynicism. In the foreground of four poems entitled "Romantic Poem I-IV," which deal with duality, are all the painful hardships and obstacles that a couple experiences. "Randol Poem," possibly one of the most sensitive in the collection, stands out due to the fact that the depicted event is not met with irony but rather intensified. Some of the poems, which were written during the holidays ("Shrovetide Poem," "Easter Poem 2004," "Assumption Poem," "September 1st," "November 1st"), point to the contrast between the idyllic atmosphere, emptied symbolism of the holiday, and harsh reality.

Upon reading a book such as this, we can state that this kind of poetry in its essence values revolt. In the case at hand, the personal and social rebellion has a solid base and does not float weightlessly in midair. Irony remains one of the key elements of *C(o)urt Interpretations*; Mustar uses it with no hesitation, and by intensifying it, achieves its opposite and eventually its annihilation. Irony, which often turns into self-irony, at times overcomes melancholic impulses; their edges are smoothed by an urge to smile. In a sense, the tone of some of Mustar's poems can be compared to that of the comics in a daily paper: both involve the urgency to update an event, criticism, irony, and humor. Yet neither the former nor the latter comes equipped with an objective recipe to guarantee its quality; it can only be a result of the right combination and an adequate dose of all the constituents, which is something only the best achieve. This, along with the collection's immediateness in terms of its contents, is why *C(o)urt Interpretations* raises dust on the shelves of modern Slovene poetry.

How can I not feel tormented
when I – a middle-aged man – am forced to wait
for my verse to mature
while the world keeps turning into science fiction.
I'm so numb
that I can't feel the mobile phone vibrating in my trouser
    pocket anymore.
The box, which at the push of a button
can also serve to entertain,
is vulturously broadcasting the funeral of the President of State.
Viewing figures go up when the camera zooms in on accident-
    charred bodies,
and the meter goes berserk
when the grieving faces of his wife and children appear on the
    TV screen.
In another country, an earthquake buries three thousand people.
The weight of casualties of war places them mere third.
The computer animation is scratching its head.
Even if we are saved from bird flu by vegetarianism,
from AIDS by sexual abstinence,
and from SARS by becoming homebodies,
we will not escape one-track-mindedness.
I receive an e-mail,
I hope it's not virus-infected,
saying that the promised land
has just embargoed the import of literature from so-called
    non-democratic countries.

depression

Should I start building my musculature in fitness centers?
Should I turn into Super, Action or Spider Man,
are you willing to become my Xena
so that together we can save the world?
Is this becoming to a poet?
How much virtual decency this indecent world requires!
I'm not sure whether I should give in,
climb the nearest hill
to watch the freshly fallen snow,
or change the channel instead,
that's why today, my dearest,
I'm so goddamn depressed.

Is it coming? Is it coming not? Is it coming? Is it coming not?
I'm counting as I clip my toenails.
It's a good thing I still have all ten toes left
and the result was negative, so I go to bed with ease.
But tonight the vultures won't fall asleep,
there's a smell of fresh coffee in the newsrooms,
even if we keep turning the lights on
we won't blind their greedy eyes,
even if we sleep at high speed we won't leave their news behind.
How can I kiss you when you bring me a fresh roll in the morning,
when a motorized paperboy serves me a fresh image of war?
This morning my coffee doesn't smell at all, there's something
    rotten in the air.
Darling, I think I'll beat my TV addiction,
a good thing it's Thursday today and the daily *Work* comes with
    the supplement "Drive –
to a Better Place."

d–night

Today I found out that art is heavy.
I saw my wife, the poet,
taking off
on an expedition to the copy store with a backpack full of books.
About 3 kilos, I assess.
I wonder how much she would get for them on Congress Square,
should the time be right for a book fair.
Oh, the backpack looks so good on her, yet she still has to
    climb Mount Triglav,
even though she makes an effort to maintain intercultural
    relations.
Fresh air will do her good.
Before she leaves I kiss her briefly.
Having a practical mind,
I shove the daily mail down her pockets,
registered mail in one, regular in the other,
so that her balance is intact, now off you go.
OK, financial difficulties have been solved,
checks are in the mail,
we won't need to sell our books.
Actually, there's only one thing that scares me – our intertextuality,
unconscious intertextuality.
I fear that she might carry a virus back home from the copy store,
which would infect my sense of protection against influences.
If all else fails I shall resort to legal practice,
everybody is innocent
until proven guilty.

apoetic poem

I will call to mind fugitives, thieves, burglars,
whores, drug dealers, rapists,
and write another 3 kilos of books.
Today, L., we don't need to sell as yet.

Gypsies grown dumb,
the bear beer is not on the menu
but they serve an excellent house specialty:
grilled Pushkin.
The chef carves him up painstakingly.
There are no manners at the Red Snake, you can eat with your
    fingers.
The poet sentenced to silence is brought innards.
The hungry ad designer bites into a juicy leg,
and to me the waiter serves the heart!
I keep chewing and chewing.
How tough post-post modernism is!

at the red snake

I murdered myself of all people.
Killed my illusions, my dreams,
and fell asleep like an angel.
On the third day I was resurrected as a court interpreter.
Where are you, Fyodor Mikhailovich, old chum,
where are you, so we can go get trashed on vodka?
My brother from an early age
who got me high without illegal substances,
stole my nights away, and caused psychosomatic disorders
back when I was still a little bear who wanted to see the stars
    up close.
Resurrect, get yourself to the bar,
bring along your imaginary gang of criminals,
and I'll bring along my real one
so we can have a vodka-drinking contest
competing as equals,
and draw the lines.
We are strong, born winners,
mine are not the kind to be conscious-stricken, I know them
    inside out.
I smell their sweaty palms in courtroom docks on a daily basis, and
I flirt with prostitutes, the only advantage of my profession.
Consciousness belongs in novels.
Verdicts in the name of the people – which people? – my dearest,
are inefficient, they don't cause internal struggles,
and consciousness only exists in a bad TV adaptation of your
    novel.

crime and punishment

Everything is an illusion, a cheap play with even cheaper actors.
I know I'm going to beat you, old chum,
I just don't know
which one of us is better off.

Ding-dong, ding-dong...
Above our little house,
which is purely fictional
since I forgot to enroll in a national housing savings scheme,
black clouds are gathering.
Ancient sages, who have long since been eaten by maggots,
would be quick to observe that there's no use crying over spilt milk,
whereas priests have never thought of
pointing out to their well-groomed congregation at Mass
that they should use less hairspray,
not to mention deodorant.
We're lying in our matrimonial bed,
flies are swarming above us,
not the science fiction kind
but indigenous Sartrean flies,
they're crawling into our ears, into our noses, they're bumping
    into the corners of our eyes,
buzzing: "Be what you are! Take no notice of others!"
There's a thunderstorm outside,
beech and oak trees are splitting in half,
crushing the heads of does beneath,
deer antlers are struck by lightning.
Poetry is going to endure without its popular themes
and we without words.
Then there's a shooting glance with a fly in the eye in place of
    the cornea,
and we're gone.

environmental poem

We're getting fat with no food,
we've stopped biting our nails,
they're getting long and pretty,
one good thing in the afterlife,
since the post-mortem award we may receive
won't even take care of our tomb.
And when the neighbors arrive, equipped with air freshener
to overcome the unbearable stench
that oozes from our decomposing bodies,
there will be a flood, my dear, the Deluge.
Noah whispered to me in my dreams
that he didn't feel like building another ark,
which will make us, whether you like it or not, the last romantics.

I'm walking around at a book fair,
countless books send twinges up my spine.
As I pass by a medical handbook stall it crosses my mind
that it's time to see the doctor again;
nothing in life is free.
If there's some *potica* up for grabs again at the cookbook stall
    this year,
I think I'll have a piece.
Life is short, but sweet. Or so they say.
I keep walking and when I catch sight of an author whose name
    is written in history,
I squash nostalgia like a cigarette butt,
at least until next year
when a professional *excessively sentimental yearning for
    return to some past period*
awaits me.
In an improvised bar nearby book dealers are stuffing themselves
    with meat balls,
washing them down with plenty of alcohol,
for book trade, too, has its classification number in the business
    register
and order forms that go with it.
Just as chills go up my spine realizing that the friend
who sponsored my work has turned into a perfect stranger,
the Little Prince taps me on the shoulder and whispers to me
that his author's bones were recently found in the ocean.
Behind him, there you are in your wedding gown.

nostalgia

Tzvetaeva and Pasternak are our best men.

Angels carry the inscription *"in medias res"*...

Dickinson catches the bouquet and Dostoevsky showers us
  with rice.

Arabella, who was late for the wedding, presents us with the
  magic ring.

I go down on my knees and slip it on your ring finger.

You twist it around and we land in the Elizabethan Period:

book sellers in rags are begging for a piece of bread,

there's a large crowd gathered around Shakespeare's stall.

Prince is saying that we're having supper after closing time.

The seller of psychological textbooks smiles affably at me.

The expression on my face must be telling her that she's found
  a good customer;

she's offering me a book on the latest findings in dealing with
  stress,

even though she must have classified me as a schizophrenic.

I decline politely saying that I've just experienced magical realism.

And once again I feel an endless wave of nostalgia for the 17th
  century.

I ask her to give me something for depression

so she sells me a handsomely illustrated book at a 10 percent
  discount.

As for my spine, it will have to wait till next year.

After a nice literary evening
I emotionally type in the wrong PIN code thirteen times in a row
and block my phone once and for all.
A charming woman's voice informs the callers
that I can't be reached at the moment.
At last I'm free
as a bird.
For such a cliché, they say, a copy writer can land no less than
    five hundred thousand.
Why on earth write poetry then?
Employers can't reach me,
I'm free indeed.
I don't care how I'm going to settle the recalculation of the
    electricity bill.
The telephone directory is erased.
When reconnected, the little gadget
will help me make an inventory of my friends.
As it sadly lacks feelings,
it will arrange them alphabetically.
Since my fingers are addicted to pressing little keys,
I'm trying to satisfy my craving with the remote control.
On one of the channels a charming middle-aged lady
is advertising a loaf of bread, *Kosovel*,
which *Mlinotest* began baking to mark the poet's anniversary.
In the background a book is reigning, the bulk of it
teeming with photographs of the author and his family,
letters, manuscripts.

free as a bird © mobitel

It, too, needs to be sold.
I have a feeling that his poetry has degenerated into
the bread crumbs that are falling on the lady's skirt.
A lump starts to form in my throat,
even though my life so far has been perfectly alright.
Like a real boy I never cry,
as a child I always played with nothing but toy cars.
I just want to be read
the way I read Kosovel.
Internally struggling, I grab the phone
and take it to the service center.
A complacently affable employee
doesn't manage to hide her sympathy
and pity
with regard to my defective memory
when she informs me that all data in the phone has been erased.
I want to tell her
that this isn't as tragic as it could be,
that sometimes even people are erased.
I don't say a word.
It's time for a personal inventory.

Unto the mattress
size 140x200 cm
worries are sprinkled and stick to our bodies.
Which one of us has forgotten to buy
the antistatic dust spray in the supermarket?
Our backs touching bashfully
persevere in silence,
only our stomachs dare to establish communication,
night butterflies are rumbling in yours,
in mine bored Jonah is throwing stones into my gall bladder.
Drink up the Biokill and kill the night moths,
give me a knife so I can rip up my belly
and twist Jonah's neck,
then snuggle up to me,
my lady Macbeth,
I'm sweeter still as a fillet.

(literary) nocturne

King Alcohol gave such a scare to Virginia Woolf
that she ran hiding in the Coliseum.
Am I to blame that the ride on the city bus
en route Airport Rd-the Mall seems like *The Hours* to me?
On trial as a perpetrator of the criminal offence
of trespassing into the world of literature according to Article 311
of the Literary Code,
I'm admiring judge robes.
A wig is all that's missing to make it a wonderful costume drama.
The court found me guilty.
I was condemned to ten years of watching
film nightmares in a multiplex cinema.
My poetic egocentricity counted as a mitigating circumstance,
while an aggravating circumstance was the fact that I spend my
    nights in bed next to the poet
who wrote unambiguously
that she was more afraid of herself than of Virginia Woolf.
Since in the case at hand the sustainable development of art is
    supposed to be jeopardized,
the court issued a secondary sentence –
a deportation from Paradise for a period of ten years.
Now I'm calmly observing poppy fields.

king alcohol

I never cared about going West.
I followed the wars in the Middle East on the TV screen,
and I finished the school of life east of the Carpathians.
The western myth sells well, more or less.
For 700 Slovene Tolars, for instance, you can see a good film
on the subject.
My cinema is a very special cinema, though, a capitalistic cinema.
A real upside-down world.
I merely watch and get paid for doing it.
The film's quality does not depend on the price.
My films are three-dimensional – you don't need special glasses,
and the bonus feature is a real-life odor,
the smell of the sweaty living bodies of those who in inhumane
circumstances
made a pilgrimage to the promised West.
The distinctive point of these films is their interactivity.
At the moment that I want to soften the harsh story line,
instill a sense of romanticism into it by saying "I love you" to
the lady judge,
there she comes through the entrance to Kosovel Hall, the
intellectual,
the quasi-film critic saying: "What a cliché!"
How unjust God is.
He has fined her for being vain,
while he pays me money just for calling up
a criminal's wife – a seventeen-year-old mother with a
three-month-old baby –

go west

in order to tell her that her husband's journey ended in jail,
and fines me with a guilty conscious.
In the world of my films there are no aesthetic categories,
every critic is tongue-tied.
The melodrama is real, so real that the husband's tears
cause a lump to form in the throat of even the most terrible cynic.
So let me invite you, the Filmologist, to my cinema,
only then will you experience a real cliché:
"Real-life stories"...

Self-respect or no self-respect,
business is business.
By market laws every little thing is worth selling,
Faust knew that already.
In my mind I take off my shoes and socks,
and with my toes that are considerably too long
I start ripping stockings
underneath ladies' solemn evening gowns.
I grab gentlemen by their ties,
and swing them around above the tables laden with delicacies.
Heaven to the brave!
In the evening, as I'm showering off
the sensations of repulsion,
I can perfectly understand
raped women seen in documentaries.
To tell you the truth, all of us can be seen gobbling over there,
the cultured and the uncultured ones.
My dear, if I could turn food into verse,
and thus become digestible at last
or get stuck in the opponent's throat,
I wouldn't be late for lunch again.

reception

My old computer went berserk,
its ventilator droned so ominously
and tore my brain to pieces
that the sounds in my bedroom made me impotent.
Last night she got up, unscrewed it and plugged it into her head.
The poor thing burned out.
The engineer who performed the autopsy
ascertained that this was a case of classical amnesia
which computers catch in their third stage of life.
Thank god, objectively speaking, neither me nor her is the murderer,
but I'm tantalized by subjective circumstances of the act,
namely that I blindly believed the Godsent
who promised me to buy it some extra memory,
and that I passively waited till the very end
without giving it a chance,
or instilling it with extra power,
as it opened my eyes,
and with the red underlining of *Spelling and Grammar*
turned my attention to the collocation "false angels."
Rest in peace!

in memoriam

How cold inspiration can be!
In the strong north wind, a British version of *Baywatch*
is desperately trying to rescue sailboats
built for active holidays.
Why on earth don't they immigrate to the warm
refuge of the Californian sun?
The sky is obtaining that particular hue of blue,
just like in the painting
of Mary, Joseph and baby Jesus
that hangs above Grandma and Grandpa's matrimonial bed,
and at which I, the city kid,
would stare depressed throughout the long summers of my
    country vacations.
Those who believe in astrology,
tell me what's truly tacky,
the painting or the sunset.
Libras are supposed to have an exquisite sense of aesthetics.
There is a red light on the mini-bar display in my hotel room.

north wind

Today I've been abandoned
by my only daughter – the scarecrow.
She left my apartment decidedly, puberty-driven,
and moved to be with her aunt – a genuine puppeteer.
She says she's fed up with everything,
that playing with round stamps
and computer games no longer satisfy her
even though I've bought a flat screen.
She's not happy with her name – Cassilda.
She's fed up with the parties I throw for her birthday.
She is mad at me because I refuse to understand her and keep
    inviting to the bashes
neat Little Red Riding Hood and the Princess with her pea.
"I'd rather sleep in an ashtray under the sink at my aunt's
than in your computer room.
Her place smells of paint and old rags,
you've got three hard disks and only one daughter
and you still couldn't choose in life."
She refuses to enrol at a university, she earns her own money now.
She makes a living scaring passers-by through a book-shop
    window.
"A book every week – of your own choice!" she snaps at me:
"You're a doctor of literature but you can't cure even a common cold!
I earn so many books I get digestive disorders!
Doctors say a change of scenery would do me good."
And indeed she left – with Yurymury to Africa –
happily ever after.

family tragedy

Do you know how tough it is to be romantic in words
after master Petrarch said it all,
and on the topic of walking barefoot hand-in-hand across
    blooming meadows
high school girls have written far and wide in their school
    compositions?
Words and objects don't count, you do know the candlestick
that Gianni bought for us is too big to fit in the car.
What matters is action.
My princess, do you remember
how I came flying through your window on a white horse,
tore you from the hold of the clerical-despotic society,
and just before we landed threw you down to the ground,
so that you could remain an autonomous poet?
Do you remember how I sat by your bed for fourteen days,
injecting cynicism in you three times a day,
and how when you got better we walked together, hand in hand,
through the woods of literary theory for four years?
You know well that I'm gentle,
and that I love you so much I bring you sauerkraut even as I write,
so much that I shall lie down next to the cabbage,
allow you to roll me in a pie, stick it in the oven and eat it.
This is what will finally make you realize
that love can thrive on food alone.

romantic poem

You see, we do know how to be romantic, my darling.
Our seats in the *cercle* are empty this evening.
Romeo and Juliet are acting out for each other.
While we're lying under the blanket next to each other
as their projection,
with a bag of chips in our hands
pushing bad news deep down into our stomachs.
Do not despair my sweetheart, the bearer of bad tidings
at our door won't ring again, I assure you.
The blues is for others.
Eye-sight is so cheap, a few hundred kilograms of chips
meaning less than a hundred hours of night shift,
and fewer bags of chips, of course.
The result: a healthy spirit in a healthy body.
I won't be bringing you any more blueberry cakes.
Let's snuggle close to each other instead,
let's push our thumbs deep into our throats
and puke up all the bad news bulimic-style.
No one can take away from us what we have.
Is this a cliché?
For the sight in one eye I already earned last Saturday.

romantic poem 2

When I told you I was an angel
you immediately asked me in the style of the Inquisition
where my wings were.
Do you really think
that Ana was built inside the church walls in vain,
and that Dorian Gray's horns were trimmed for nothing?
Do you know how tough it is to be an angel in Bucharest for
    Christmas?
In these new crazy times when the aged little Parisian
went nuts again and started to wear exaggerated makeup.
She put on thousands of little light-bulbs and with the power of
220 watts killed stray dogs,
and shut homeless kids, high on glue vapors, in the gutters
and subway tunnels – all for beauty.
She's adorned herself with *fast foods*,
she serves eggplant salad with extra mayonnaise to make it
    more *à la française*
in pretty plastic containers.
How shall I put a stop to queues of people swarming at the
    Christmas-New Year's Fair?
How shall I be a prophet when I serve you salad *bonjour* for a
    romantic dinner?

romantic poem 3

At the Immigration Office I found out
that love is empirically provable.
What you need is the following documents and pieces of evidence:
birth certificate, it means we exist;
marriage certificate, we signed our love;
statement of non-conviction, you're clean as a whistle, you won't
    kill me;
proof of income and assets, I love you as bread alone;
proof of lodging, no more romance under the stars.
The theoretical test of endurance is followed by a practical one:
a queue at the registry office;
a queue in court;
a queue in the bank as the computer system collapses;
a queue at the land registry office.
As I stand bare naked, you can't be as naked even on your
    wedding night,
with verified identity, means and emotions on paper
in a queue in front of the above-mentioned office,
I instantly forget all about the following queues from my past:
a queue to buy bread at the privately owned bakery;
an even/odd queue at the military medical check-up;
a queue at the Student's Office;
a queue in literary translation.
Now that I'm finally acquainted with all the synonyms of the
    word *lawful*,
I can say to you on the basis of all worldly and holy sacraments:
I love you!

romantic poem 4

P.S.: My dear, the queue to sign the marriage license in front of the door marked "Weddings" was the sweetest.

Just as I was beginning to think
that my sensitivity had reached its peak,
friendly people pointed out it was nothing but a neurosis.
To hell with army medical staff
who wrote
that I'm a hypersensitive personality with neurotic reactions,
which began my process
of turning into an author with all the rights attached.
After civil society had proclaimed my actions a risk for the
    environment,
it took immediate action through its representative – my
    neighbor the joiner.
He lay me down on the working area of a circular saw and
    made a cut.
He carefully separated both halves of the brain.
While yin women were picking the left half, representatives of
    yang were doing the right.
The latter were soon out of work.
Diligent yin workers were much more successful.
They soon picked a bucketful of nerve endings
woven through and through with old grudges, mental pains,
    and similar junk.
They preserved the heart in formaldehyde with care,
and set the jar under the counter
so that it wouldn't get broken, for it should continue to serve
    me for a long time coming.
If you die of cancer, you are free

sensitive poem

to display your charity in daily press,
denouncing the décor on your grave,
but I'm in for a spiritual death.
When the work was done, it was time for the seamstress,
who lives at the end of the street, to kindly give me a patching job.
Then her daughter took me to the mobile phone store
to verify whether I'm finally sane enough to buy a user's package
which comes with a gift – a CD.
I failed.
Since there's absolutely nothing in the head, a heart attack
    followed.

P.S.: I forgot to state in my will that I denounce wreaths and
candles to the benefit of the Society of Cardiovascular Disease
Patients.

My body has broken down.
Vintage *teran* and peasant's feasts have assaulted my liver
while nerves and worries have begun to peck at my stomach
 like ravens.
They nip at it causing internal boiling,
yet I still attack it with introspection.
Seeing that it can't punch me in the face,
my body assaults on the inside like a regular enemy
causing bleedings in my mouth with pyorrhoea.
It has forced me into examining my own shit each day
and carrying it to the diagnostic lab for a check-up if necessary.
Everything is in the head, they say.
The doctor orders me to tidy up my attic
or she's going to refer me for a gastroscopy.
Turks used to impale people from the outside
while here on doctor's note, in the name of science, we're being
 impaled from the inside.
You said I was being blasphemous when I said
relationships needn't be blessed.
I'm Judas, my darling, who renounced not only Jesus,
I'm Judas who renounced not only another,
I'm Judas who renounced his own self.
In the evenings when I'm alone with my TV
and the old box doesn't let me get a word in edgeways
going on and on about wars,
and the lump in my stomach is on the rise again,
I wish to be referred for a lobotomy

diagnosis

to have all the cells in charge of sensitivity destroyed

so I could eat pork legs and drink *teran* again.
On the "Midnight Club" talk-show right after "News Echo"
they said love is just a tiny bit,
that one can't live on it alone, that one needs to work,
work for partnership –
so let's get down to it, my darling.
Since I'm refused a lobotomy
a bowel examination is upon me,
a homosexual act also in the name of science,
so let's get down to it, quick!

In the hour of truth, my wife
assisted by St. George who came riding in a Clio,
nailed a shoddy pietà on the wall,
and now Virgin Mother of God is threatening
to murder me during the Holy Communion,
even though it was me who had bought her a glass frame,
which cracked due to her oversized ego.
Today I threw away postal orders
with which I used to play as a child,
and paid my bills over a bank-by-phone.
Let me eat the flesh,
it's not Friday today,
and even a dog likes to eat in peace,
isn't that right, pietà?
I turned my dreams into an office,
I replaced toy trains with the keyboard
and the captain hat with ring binders.
Tomorrow I shall go to sea
as a true captain without a ship,
lone wolf,
a fan of *The Old Man and the Sea*,
on his own and of all the rest
in equal proportion,
as someone who values himself just enough
to refuse to be sold at public auction –
if you don't want to protect me on land, then protect me at sea,
oh, Holy Virgin, I give myself wholly to thee.

the truth

Grandpa, as I was looking for the grill today
which was concealed behind the proud gas burner tripod,
I laid my eyes on the walnut tree which Grandma in her will
had never left to my self-publishing uncle.
Do you see how deep folk wisdom is?
As I'm replenishing the fire with dry twigs and everything
    smells so nice
I can see you again in the coffin lowered into the ground,
while Grandma, unaware of being a patron of Art,
was incinerated against her wishes.
I'm burning dry walnut leaves in memory of her.
Today it's only the smoke that makes my eyes water.
My lyricism has gone under with you.
It dripped away during those three days
while I was watching your dead shriveled body
which didn't swell one bit.
This left village slanderers without their favorite subject,
and coffin-bearers with no need to exercise their muscles.
I don't know what it was that flies found so dear on the ossified body.
Grandpa, when Grandma was buried
I was wearing sunglasses,
but she never got to where you are,
since a hole no deeper than thirty centimeters is enough to bury
    an urn.
The last time she could hold your hand was on the catafalque,
and this was the last melodramatic scene that brought tears to
    my eyes.

randol poem

I'm not going to attend the mass held on the anniversary of
   your death,
I'm going to grab hold of a chainsaw,
cut up the walnut tree, build a bonfire and disinfect the air,
burn up all the excessive words, destroy the last buds of lyricism.

Empty promises made by the artist
are flying across the pristine clean kitchen
and keep turning into mayflies, each with a day to live,
dying by the heat of a dull light.
On the table some materials instead of food.
A copyright agreement has lost its way and ended up
among court records yet to be bound.
It has found its place between a denunciation
and an inventory of confiscated objects.
Records, who is going to bind you?
God, me, or the criminal court?
I'm discovering that I was enjoying my pigsty of a kitchen more.
There I was feeding cockroaches with dirt
and reading books still damp from the flood
caused by clogged drainpipes,
and feces were swimming in the apartment
like fish in the aquarium.
Contract, watch out for me,
I'm holding scissors in one hand,
and the red tape in the other.
While the artist keeps talking and talking...

poem on survival

When my personal physician
was reading the X-ray picture of my ribs,
she was horrified.
Wormwood between the ribs!
After that she touched my head.
My ego immediately swelled
and my head turned into a balloon.
She took my hand
and together we flew up to the sky.
She kept taking X-ray pictures of angels like crazy,
while I was plucking wormwood from my ribs.

Just then another miracle occurred.
When a leaf of wormwood fell to the ground it turned into a brick,
and so I began to build the Tower of Babel:
layer upon layer and brick by brick...
I was a regular Sisyphus in a frenzy.
When we reached the top the doctor spoke nothing but Latin,
while God made me tongue-tied once and for all.
He knocked me to the ground and chained me down with
     commandments,
for each commandment a pair of chains.
Oh, sweet Christian suffering!

airborne

"Our life is *in medias res* poetry,"
I'm roused by this sentence of yours
as I'm failing to drop a coin into a shopping cart
in front of a supermarket in Italy.
Like a complex-ridden *schiavo* I glance around.
Has anyone noticed my lack of consumer skills?
Complexes derive from old footwear
which we used to discard in garbage containers.
I finally manage to set the cart free.
What a cheap freedom!
Shakespeare is the one who said
life was theatre, isn't he?
I grope in my pocket.
My precious, heavenly blue Eurocard,
which gives me a sense of security, is still there.
I enter the shopping temple self-confidently.
Theatre, darling, our life is *in medias res* theatre.
Forget Beckett! Forget Ionesco!
I snap the trembling fingers of an entrance exam candidate
for the Academy of Theatre – Department of Theatre Directing,
and with magical realism I turn the products into female
    characters of Mazilu's dramas.
They're surrounding me, smearing tasty stuff on me,
they're eating it off me!
Don't be jealous, darling,
It's all fiction anyway.
At the cash register, suspicious looks from the cashier.

in medias res

I take the Eurocard out of my pocket and threaten
to cut her throat if she refuses
to reiterate lines from the drama "Fools in Moonlight" until
    she goes into a trance.
My co-spenders tap me on the shoulder,
it's time to go.
In the car, the purchases have to be separated carefully
so we don't steal from each other.
As we're driving to the border the adrenaline is pumping,
within me a trembling boy awakens
who used to smuggle Brooklyn chewing gum in his pocket.
Border, border, bordeeeeeeer...
For those I care about
I never buy presents in shops.
And this, darling, is for our anniversary.

When I bump into a typical family
on my way to the shopping mall on a Sunday,
it gives me the shudders.
Father, mother, a couple of adorable kids in their Sunday best
holding balloons they were given at a presentation of who-
  knows-what miraculous product.
If I was to meet them years ago
on their way back from Sunday Mass,
the expressions on their faces would have been exactly the same,
only the girl would be wearing blue sandals and white stockings,
and the boy's socks would be gray with a tartan pattern.
Another difference is certain.
In the confession booth they surely won't dare to admit
that they are in favor of Sunday store opening hours.
Any basic psychology textbook will tell you
that biological needs are primary human needs.
I elbow my way through the balloons and stoned faces.
When I pass the first row of shelves, I'm through with any
  possible desire for lyricism,
exploration of language, and postmodernism too.
Verse never flows as quickly as items flow into a cart.
A bonus in poetry? Forget about it!
Only when I see friendly aunty Cruella De Vil,
who sells macrobiotic bread,
I begin to empty my cart in the spirit of salvation.
I don't ask her about the fur,
I bring my biological needs to the express-5-items-or-less lane.
But what about the spiritual ones?

ah, our daily existence

Brainwashed, I take my spring-loaded rubber stamp
and make my last imprint.
Imported barroom dancers will be free to work again,
fat drooling capitalists will have a chance to light up their nights.
My fee will buy us theatre tickets.
Yesterday my cousin took his bull to the slaughterhouse to be
    branded,
even though he's a butcher himself.
A blue brand on a skinned leg is a guarantee against madness.
This year we bought 20 kilos.
Packaging time is here again.
It's best to use two bags for the soup parts
as the bones can easily pierce the first bag,
and that is supposedly not healthy
because air gets in.
Father doesn't get home from work till the afternoon.
He can cut the steaks in such a way
that they're nice and tender afterwards.
Meat and bones for the soup will make 20 packages or so.
For twenty Sundays, the good old soup will come before sautéed
    potatoes,
for a good five months there will be peace in my pious homeland,
no Chinese food will be allowed to disturb the standard pace,
intervene in prearranged conversations and interrupt the
    polka beat.
There will be peace, peace and quiet, and we shall all be the same,
just like at Sunday Mass when we shake our hands mechanically.

branding

In my mind I'm scheming a subversive discourse
which is bound to shake up the Sunday laden table.
A starting-point will be a conversation on
how the Muslims eat beef too,
pork is problematic, and probably blood sausages,
how they too shake hands, every time they meet no less,
how the church and the mosque have something in common –
the church tower, the *turn*, as we say.
When I start to make steak packages, a drop of blood runs
    down my arm,
and a literary motif of love,
and probably of nature too, slips through my fingers.
Everything, everything is under control.
And Big Brother is nothing but an entertainment program.

A week before Shrovetide I began to skin myself.
I started with my neck,
making gentle little cuts with a kitchen knife,
in order to sell the skin at a flea market.
I left the fat on to make the fur coat warmer, more expensive.
On a Shrove Saturday I'm lying in my bed,
skinned, merely muscular and handsome
I'm waiting to pay off maskers,
who bring good luck to a home they visit,
with the money I earned.
My computer warns me
that the operation was aborted by the user.
And the maskers are nowhere to be seen.
As I fall asleep, a mountain of books collapses from the shelves.
They avoid me as if I were a leper,
forming a beautiful mound.
The Fates surround me
and foretell my happy death in unison.
Then Cinderella jumps down from the shelf,
giving me a lethal graze on my forehead
that leaves a scar.
Long after the Ash Wednesday neighbors' thoughts were the
    same –
the death and the funeral were beautiful.

shrovetide poem

This year a statistical deviation in the calculation of holidays
    has seen to it
that ecumenism extends beyond the calendar.
In Alaska they've figured out
which came first
– chicken or egg –
and started to dye chickens.
On the Old Continent,
Kinder eggs and kitschy Easter eggs
make my eyes hurt.
Similarly multicolored were the sleeping pills taken by the
    young writer
who had never in her life read Aristotle's *Poetics*.
When I was reading her work I believed
that she was the only human being in the world
still able to find the fountain of eternal youth.
She was thrust into an untimely grave by her distrust of modern
    cosmetic concoctions.
Chemistry prevented her from dying dramatically.
She didn't drown like Ophelia.
She fell asleep on the shore with soaked ankles,
and her Hamlet, as if she'd been Cinderella,
first, in terror, found her shoes.
Ethnologists advocate the natural dying of eggs
with onion skins.
This year Christ died on the cross in vain again,
while Aglaya's words are ressurecting with a vengeance.

easter poem 2004

Thank you, Mother of God,
for letting me lie in front of the TV in peace today
and nonchalantly switch the channels.
Thank you for the day off work
so that I can be quasi-depressed once again
because you took to the sky,
having been afraid of Peter Pan throughout my childhood.
Children's literature is curable,
now I'm threatened by literature for adults.
I'm suffering from a lack of symbolism and metaphors.
I'm watching you
as you march at the head of the procession,
flattened out on an icon,
or voluptuous in the style of Michelangelo.
You're able to materialize tears
which no one wants to see,
for the canon is what it is.
There's a literary one, too, you know.
El Greco is to blame since it was he
who took the eastern canon to the West
and caused a commotion.
He's the main culprit
that worshipers' attention is drawn towards your appearance.
"You Are Beautiful, Oh Flower Mary..."
Metaphorically speaking,
the icon would easily knock off the head of the statue:
thousands of little pieces of glass and gravel
would rise up to the sky
and life would be one big holiday.

assumption poem

The city streets have turned blue
with the police uniforms
in charge of getting the children to school safely,
whereas little Metka
instead of having a yellow kerchief tied around her neck
was dressed in a green coat
and had her kidney removed.
Through her veins, instead of her first cocoa from the cafeteria,
chemicals are flowing in order to root out the insidious disease.
This is really not a good time for religion classes in the curriculum.

september 1st

After having successfully traded
Pizzeria Triglav for Pizzeria Napoli
and Istria for South Dalmatia,
we are strolling hand in hand
through a national park.
Despite all the splendors of nature,
my fingers aren't reaching for a ball-point pen.
Instead, with a Tarzan-like strength,
I'm defending the big city girl from nature's wonders.
The heavenly calm is shattered by yodelling compatriots on
    an office outing
who, after just a couple of beers, are warbling Dalmatian songs
    like nightingales.
Among the fir needles,
a heroin needle glistens.

holiday poem

The city and the buses reek of greenery.
Personifying the love of the dead,
chrysanthemums have lost all charm.
In graveyards, new coats,
meticulously groomed hairstyles,
new gravel,
candles that burn for a week.
An ikebana contest is next:
neighbors, look how much we loved them!
A few days before All Saints' Day
Grandma is going on her last journey –
to Grandpa.
Will they reunite at the right time,
instilling some sense into the absurd holiday?
On the tombstone, Grandpa's name is carved in gold.
It's only proper that Grandma also gets letters like that,
a poor consolation in the moments of terror right before death.
Farewell, Granny,
you know I'm not a vulture
but when I'm in the neighborhood –
not on a holiday like this, that's for sure,
when it's on I lock myself behind three locks in the apartment –
I'll come by, I promise,
but with no candles or chrysanthemums, of course.

november 1st

I'm going to kill you and bury you in my garden.
This will be our Day of the Dead.
I will gently light candles for you,
thirty-one candles,
just like on your birthday.
Our cake will be flower arrangements
smelling of periwinkle.
I'll wait for my fangs to grow,
to sharpen,
and then I'll kiss you – on the neck.
Eviva Transylvania.

day of the dead

The singing of Christmas carols
in a hundred-year-old yet vital church.
Gregorian chants give
wings to singers
and they take off.
And then it strikes,
the earthly superpower strikes
and transforms the alter into a Coca Cola can,
wrapping the church in red paper with golden snowflakes,
and binding it firmly with a festive tie.
Red hoods are flying through the air,
Father Christmas turns into Mother Christmas,
angelic singers with sodden wings –
a proof that carbonated drinks aren't refreshing –
are jumping out of the can and falling helplessly to the ground
singing Jingle Bells.
A petrified bishop, engraved in a church pillar,
splits in two.
Angels expelled from Eden take each other's hands and form a
     semicircle,
doomed to eternal singing about the dreams of a white Christmas.
God's punishment has no effect though,
holier-than-thou church ladies continue to lie only outside the
     church walls.

christmas poem

A village behind God's back, with no tacky décor,
is being scourged by the wind from hell.
The priest politically interweaved sins
into his Midnight Mass sermon,
which makes them seem relative.
The composition took him so long
that he forgot to drop by the house of a junkie on a rebound.
And I still claim that God is not ours or yours alone,
you can't hold a referendum to determine his existence.
I sweep away the tradition.
Instead of Grandma's dove-decorated pie
there are pancakes with factory-made marmalade on the table,
and I ignore them.
When I'm looking for scrap wood,
which will drive away the cold,
at the island's colorful scrap heap –
even in Europe, decorated for Christmas, no such colors can
    be found –
I accidentally come upon pieces of my identity.
Cheeky parts were hidden right at the bottom of a bag full of
    kitchen waste,
and I've nearly collapsed from tiresome rummaging.
When I split in half again during the Christmas dinner,
the reincarnated Pope watchfully oversees the table.
Tomorrow we shall go and embrace new victories

christmas poem 2

Congratulations! Condolences!
Greeting cards are always ugly in the same way
regardless of the design: a bunch of flowers or a black ribbon.
Clichés in sentences cut through the heart like surgeon's knives.
A complacent company dealing in catalogue sales
presents me with a gift coupon.
A well-read marketing expert hasn't forgotten to include lines
    from Wordsworth
closely followed by good wishes
for a nice celebration and much joy in the use of the discount.
As soon as the fax machine gets as smart
as mobile phones
and starts responding with the Happy Birthday tune
I shall commit suicide.

happy birthday to me

Since a brief review of world literature is running
through my mind, chockfull of academic junk,
I'm battling with an internal struggle –
postmodern frailty versus lyrical ejaculation.
It's a tie.
In my mind, I kiss my brothers, literary freemasons, on the
    forehead.
Greetings, Beckett, who art my brother, let me kiss your forehead,
    brother,
greetings, Ionesco, who art my brother, let me kiss your
    forehead, brother,
and so on and so forth...
Brothers, your legacy is flowing through my work,
even though I've never asked for it,
nor have I posthumously sued you for a statutory share.
An overload causes my internal organs to fall ill,
just as state organs are calling me to duty.
In Srebrenica, rotten corpses are being dug out again.
There's nothing left of them or after them,
legacy doesn't make any sense.
Only wandering souls are screaming again in a deserted house
    in a nearby village.
No one can stop the screaming, not the police nor the firemen
    nor the Muslim priest.
I turn off the TV and start to compile a response to the lawsuit
which my relatives, the vultures, dissatisfied with the quantity
    of legacy,

legacy

filed after Grandma died.

Blood is water.

I shall give answers to my attorney in an utterly silent voice

so that Grandma can't hear us

and won't feel the need to haunt us, having toiled enough during
her lifetime.

And us two, my dear,

to whom shall we pass on the fruits of our labor?

Shall we turn sterile in the name of art?

Come, let me kiss you

so that our lives can become *in medias res* poetry.

I'm storming through the city streets
in a hurry to get to the stationery shop
where the film ribbon for fax machines is sold.
My Panasonic ran out of it today,
which makes him beep imploringly like a pet would,
if a phobia didn't prevent one from finding shelter under our roof.
Actually, the fax machine is entirely harmless,
it's just the ribbon that needs to be replaced every two months.
I might consider getting a cactus.
An excessively complacent salesman steals my valuable time.
We're both products of a nation
whose prevalent self-image has to do with diligence.
I don't smile back at him,
I'd rather save the smile for my clients.
As I pass by the soup kitchen
which has been turned into a private school,
a vacuum blows inside my head.
Am I depressed or merely sensitive?
Or is it that I have a subconscious kind of depression
which was the subject of an article in a family magazine?
The kind which is successfully treated with electroshocks
combined with psychotherapy?
I can't make up my mind.
If I was to get electroshocks,
my productivity would surely decrease!
I run to the nearby bakery to get some bread,
devoting 25% of my smiling energy to the aged saleswoman,

no title

then I hurry back to my office.
As soon as I open the door I hear intolerable beeping.
I edge closer on tiptoes,
I open it gently and insert the ribbon.
My Panasonic emits a grateful tinkle and then falls silent –
another working day is upon us.

Loaded with the complete opus
of Shakespeare the Great,
I'm searching for inspiration in the sterile park of an Eastern
   metropolis
which is tarnished here and there by little Gypsies,
mutilated for the sole purpose of
increasing their market value,
by dislodged grandmothers whose grandchildren have stormed
   West
and forgotten to send rent and bread money,
and by some more similar atrocities on show.
Cheeky pigeons are flying just above my head,
inside it sparrows are shrieking,
an old man to my left and I are turning our heads in unison
to observe sparsely dressed young women,
fledgling dandies in moccasins with laptops on their shoulders,
legless and armless cripples.
An overdose of inspiration, I say to myself,
you'd better do a good deed,
I turn around and talk to the old man,
I feel immense self-satisfaction,
Caritas personified,
I've opened a book of wisdom on two legs,
I keep listening and listening...
Too many motifs! Too much inspiration!!!
It's not like I'm picking blueberries!

in search of inspiration

aleš mustar was born in 1968 in Ljubljana, Slovenia. He studied English and Pedagogy at the University of Ljubljana, and has a PhD in Romanian literature from the University of Bucharest, Romania. Mustar is freelance poet and translator, rendering Romanian and Macedonian literature into Slovenian. During the day, Mustar wins his bread as a court interpreter. This "double life" provides the poet with an excellent opportunity – he does not need to search for inspiration in remote places, as interesting themes and (anti-) heroes reach him in the courtroom everyday. Mustar's poems have been published in all the most important Slovenian literary magazines, and have been translated into Czech, Serbian, Polish, Macedonian, English, and Romanian. His debut collection, *C(o)urt Interpretations*, was nominated for the top Slovenian poetry prize in 2005. In addition to his poetic output, Mustar has also written texts for experimental theater performances that have been staged in Slovenia.

manja maksimovič entered the world of literary translation when she translated "My Love Is Like a Red, Red Rose" into Slovenian one day during lunch for her little sister's school assignment. After four years of English language and journalism studies, her translation jobs were no less random and varied until her friend Aleš Mustar started to write poetry. Everything that she might have discovered about his intimate world while translating his poems, she vows never to reveal.

biographies

Printed in the United Kingdom
by Lightning Source UK Ltd.
128451UK00001B/7-135/P